ON THE OTHER SIDE
OF THE WINDOW

By Marianne Szlyk

With love and gratitude to my husband, Ethan Goffman who has encouraged me in so many ways, as well as to Callie and Thelma McKay who have brought nature into our house

Thank you to friends, family, and colleagues on Facebook and in real life for your support and encouragement as well, especially to Catfish McDaris, Mary Jo Balistreri, Angelee Deodhar, Ndaba Sinabada, Will Mayo, Claudine Nash, Elizabeth Bruce and Michael Oliver, Bea Garth, Tess and Casseau Gee, Kiane Thomas, Joanna Howard, Allyson Lima, Lynne S. Viti, Chani Zwibel Butler, Yoby Henthorn, Mendes Biondo, Tamara Safford, Stacie Marinelli, John MacDonald, David Churchill, Joan Dobbie, Celia Young, and Felino A. Soriano

Thank you to Kerfe Roig for creating the work of art that became my cover.

Thank you to Amy Goffman for taking the back photo one afternoon in Staunton, VA.

Also to Dr. Michael Anthony Ingram and Dr. Mary Stone Hanley who led the workshop where I learned about counted verse (many of the poems in this book follow this format)

Contents

Looking out at Eaarth

Easter 2116 3
She Wonders What Will Become of This City 5
Crape Myrtle in East Rockville 6
Birch Tree in New England 7
What I Found Among the Reeds 8
We Disaster Tourists Travel to the Salton Sea 10
Sophia, What Might Have Been 11
The Drought Close to Home 13
At the Library of Water 14
The Library of Air 16

Nature on the Other Side of the Glass

Nature on the Other Side of the Glass 19
At the Water's Edge 20
To Eat the Rowan's Fruit 21
Mother at the Town Beach 22
January Trees 24
Abandoned 25
Maryvale Park in July 26
Seaweed on the Beach 27
Looking Out to Spectacle Island in April 28
After Miles Davis' Amandla 29
The Day Before the Bridge Closed 30
Birch Trees in North Carolina 31
Savannah in January 32
The Blooms of Fall 33
The Still Lives in Season 34
Under the Sign of Ash 35
Rock Creek Park 36
Blue Green and Brown (Rothko 1952) 38

Between Two Worlds

Between Two Worlds 41

Before the Last Days. 42

Coleus 44

At Low Tide 45

The Poet Charlotte Smith Drives Away 47

The Poet of Spotsylvania 49

Waleje for Caroline. 50

Evening on Washington Street. 53

Alternative History in Staunton, Virginia. 54

The Last Days of Fusion 55

Tonic. 57

Visiting the Ancestors. 58

Home from the Oncologist. 59

At Bonaventure Cemetery 61

Listening to Robert Glasper 62

Let's Go Away for Awhile 63

The Jazz Harpist on a Sunday Afternoon. 65

Always Looking at the Past, Sometimes Living by the River

Rocky Mountain High 69

Returning to Jamaica Pond 70

One Spring Morning at the Historic Icehouse 71

Rothko on Portland Street 73

The Space Between 74

When Words Are Stones 76

The Painter Dreams of Nevadaville, Colorado 78

In Pale November 80

For My Ex-Husband's Twin Sons

Summer 1996 82

The Last Summer without Air Conditioning 83

For My Ex-Husband's Twin Sons
Summer 1997 85
Ms. Hawthorn 86
Narrow 87
At Mile Zero on SR 26 88
The Summer After the Bridge Closed 89
Dreams of Lafayette 90
I Don't Remember the Willamette 91
Riding into Charles Street Station 93
Lafayette, September 11, 2001 95
Acknowledgements 97

Looking out at Eaarth

Eaarth is environmental writer and activist Bill McKibben's term for our planet during the process of climate change.

Easter 2116

Among the late-afternoon walkers in the square,
I tighten the hood around my pale face

and squint through goggles for
any scrap of sun that squeezes through.

I could be on Bradbury's Venus on the sweltering day
when the sizzling rain pauses, but I am on Eaarth.

In the absence of wind, showers, and past birdsong, I hear
my robe swishing. I will myself

not to think about music, my own earworms,
or suggestions sent to me like headaches.

I hear only the buzz of mosquitoes, balked by the heavy cloth.
Shuffling, weighed down, I watch holograms hover

over the stones of the square that resist ceaseless rain and wind.
The holograms show skin, unlike the living.

Mosquitoes will not bite them. They have no blood to poison.
Holograms do not talk to me. I am too poor and homely.

They are as silent as the electric cars and aircraft
that swarm the city and beyond.

I walk to the shore of the acid ocean, the beach
lacquered with toxic jellyfish and seaweed.

I smell nothing. I have been walking
here forever in search of something.

A hologram in cargo shorts floats above
like a new-age Jesus going out to Peter's boat.

I look out to the horizon. The waters cover the cities
where, as children, the holograms wore Easter outfits

and couples sauntered out in the sweetly-scented sun
so many years ago as music played from transistor radios.

The rain will resume. The music will as well.
For now, I enjoy their absence.

She Wonders What Will Become of This City

The sky above swells into a bruise over a blood vessel.
Swarms of mosquitoes rise from puddles and gutters.

It is always about to rain, sometimes about to thunder.
Acid rain cannot cleanse the ground or the air.

The pages of books dampen and thicken,
becoming too heavy to turn, too blurred to read.

The green fuzz of moss grows over trees
like plaque on teeth. Bones ache with decay.

Buses stall. Last year today would have been Code Red.
No one walks. No one rides for free.

She wonders what will become of this city
once the oceans rise and ghost towns form like coral reefs.

The real coral reefs will have crumbled,
all color leaching away into the corrosive sea.

She wonders if the people huddling miles inland
will ever visit the abrasive waters

and imagine what might have been
in the ghost town where she now sits.

Or will they avoid the scouring waves
and build their lives on mountains, now islands

above the waters, above the swarms of mosquitoes,
above the trash of daily life in a ghost town?

Crape Myrtle in East Rockville

In each yard, lavender, white, and scarlet
spring up like bouquets in children's drawings.

These trees never grew this far north before. Yet now
they color my neighborhood when roses and lilies wilt.

Someday kudzu will compete with ivy for my neighbors' fences,
for the yards of abandoned houses, for the trunks of trees.

In all seasons, palmetto palms will flourish. Away from acidic winds,
Spanish moss will hang from branches.

The people still living here will keep banana trees
on their porches. Brave neighbors will pick

the finger-sized fruit for breakfast, a curiosity
like this crape myrtle once was.

Birch Tree in New England

For every crape myrtle or towering magnolia we gain,
we lose one birch tree:

The slender stroke of titanium white
among the muddy browns and greens of summer;

The backbend held above the vernal pool
bitter with generations of oak leaves;

The leaves, yellow or green, dance
like wind chimes over the insects' drone;

The taste of birch beer—
afternoons spent foraging for wintergreen

following trails uphill
away from houses and highways

puzzling over stone walls and apple trees
in the woods that no one seemed to own.

What I Found Among the Reeds

The reeds conceal
the wetland that remains.
Smooth stalks protect
algae, frogs, birds
and hide
the swallow of water.

The bus labors
through heat and humidity
from early morning to
past exhausted, orange dusk.

When I walk,
the reeds reveal
a turtle, black nub
on a rain-slicked log
in water the color
of copper
left to the elements.

The reeds reveal
the wet stench of life,
sour mud, honeysuckle,
sulfur mixed with exhaust,
grease, and perfume.

Birds chirp and pulse
above low traffic.
The bus is electric;
it runs silently today.

Then I see
behind the reeds:
faded bottles and cans,
the torn,
black bag
blossoming
in the water.

We Disaster Tourists Travel to the Salton Sea

Last year's flowers stand,
sun-bleached kindling for the fire
about to happen here.

Blue sky flames, a torch
in the earth's hands. The sun is
the white-hot center.

No one smokes. Engines
do not idle. Air effaces
smells of death and life.

All that remains in
the sea's heart will never quench
the flames we wait for.

We wait, take small sips
of bottled water, then wait
some more. We tourists

fly from disaster
to disaster, our quick flights
adding fuel to the flames.

Sophia, What Might Have Been

She tends her lawn of rocks and cacti,
the grass and flowers long since dead,
the fruit and avocado trees brittle sticks
cut down, bundled, and left at the curb.

On the other side of a magnifying glass,
the sun scrutinizes her.
She sniffs. She coughs. She scans
the mountains for smoke.
It is always creeping into her poems,
her dreams, her hair, her clothes

although she tells herself that
what she sees is just haze.
She will not have to leave home.
She will not have to sleep
among strangers.

Still she tastes her fears,
the black that bitters,
the hiss in the garden.

There is nothing more to burn,
nothing more.
All of her writing hides in the cloud
with the books and music
she loves most.
She has long since lived alone.
There is nothing left to burn.

Sipping bottled water
from Minnesota, a package
a college friend has sent her,
she remembers his letter,
her house, herself.

There is always something left to burn.

The Drought Close to Home

So close to the sea, the Scituate reservoir
contracts to shards of clouds and sky.
Smashed on thick mud, these shards
shrink from the tree trunks and stones
rising where water once flowed.

Humid air promises rain but does not
release it. Blue sky persists
though towering clouds form.
No storms arise,
even rumors of thunder
off the coast.

Afternoon sun
grinds the shards to dust.

At the Library of Water
After Roni Horn's permanent installation

Cloudy white, beige, and yellow
columns occupy this open hall,
so much unlike the dark, untidy stacks
of a library of books.
Not solid like marble,
these columns let light shine through.
In even rows, they take up space
that study carrels would.

The only words in this library
materialize on the floor,
the way great men's names and faces
once did: Shakespeare, Dante,
Vergil, Ovid, Homer, and so on.
These words in Icelandic and English
indicate weather phenomena,
something less personal
than a man who lived and died
or his footnoted works that one reads in
dog-eared, highlighted paperback.

But all of us, even the common woman,
the common reader,
even Samuel Johnson,
experience the weather.

Still she wonders what a Californian,
a refugee from burnt hills and dry wells,
would make of this library,
the columns of what her state is missing,

a luxury fetish like caviar
or extreme thinness
in the era of cheesy fries,
corn syrup, and unlimited soda pop.

And what would a Floridian--
someone whose city is melting,
dissolving in brown water--
make of these columns
prizing water as if it were scarce,
as if it weren't drowning
his city, his street, his home.

The Library of Air
after Roni Horn's Library of Water

Where is the library of air, she asks,
turning to the enormous windows
and the brilliant sun, the clarity
that heightens each blade of grass,
each grain of sand.

She remembers
her grandparents' never-opened
can of New Hampshire air.
She remembers
rolling down the car window
to breathe in Maine
and getting a lungful of exhaust
instead.

She imagines being a visitor
from the Chinese city of Harbin
traveling to the library of air,
looking for the column of
orange and brown cloud,
its sulfur contained by glass,
which is her air, and finding
these transparent columns,
these words not in her language,
these pockets of air
that someone else, some
English-speaker, some
Icelandic-speaker
can breathe.

Nature on the Other Side of the Glass

Nature on the Other Side of the Glass

after Charles Mingus' "Mood Indigo"

As the train extracts itself from
Trenton, New Jersey, it follows clouds
south to the city of humidity
and dress codes. I watch the sky,
ignoring the ground with green leaves
I can't place and greige buildings
smeared with graffiti. The train ambles
past, following the rhythm of brush
strokes. Jaki Byard's piano on YouTube
splashes. If I were on the
other side of this glass,
I could feel water's wet kiss on
my forearm. Instead, it reminds me
how long it will be until twilight
when I emerge from this train.
Only then will I smell raindrops
on asphalt and feel indigo air.

At the Water's Edge
after Cezanne, "At the Water's Edge" (c. 1890)

Resisting the hot wind, this house at the water's edge
retreats beneath the whir of trees.

Their dry brushstrokes are blue like water or sky
and green as the end of spring.

But mostly they are the colors
of canvas, earth, and parched leaves.

The sky is a haze of brushstrokes, a wash of turpentine,
smoke to the water's edge.

Hills loom behind the house;
they are mirages made of thinned paint.

More buildings appear, shimmers in the haze,
reflections in the water.

No swimmer, no boat breaks the surface,
more mirror for land and sky than home for fish and weeds.

But the house's heart is dark and sweet
with sage and lavender, with the scent of grass and lake

protecting its guests from the hot wind, the drought,
and the smoke to the water's edge.

To Eat the Rowan's Fruit

The rowan is the sign of the thinker,
its fruit as bitter and seedy as thought.
Thin, orange pulp barely covers the pit.
Birds and deer avoid the rowan's berries,
eating them last, after the frost.

I once knew someone who claimed
to have eaten this fruit.
It was something to tick off his list
like the juniper berries he smoked
or the rainforest he later visited.

One must boil the fruit, strain it
through cheesecloth, sugar it,
ferment it, or serve it
as a jelly with gout-giving game.

But he never mentioned
how bitter
or seedy
the rowan's fruit was
as if he had gulped it down,
without thought.

Mother at the Town Beach

You don't want to swim here.
The weeds won't drag you down
to where you gulp greeny-
brown water instead of air.
They won't bind you to the bottom.
You're not drunk
like the boys who drown.

Those weeds may not
even graze you
with your short legs
as you flutter-kick above.
But there are weeds.

The water is cleaner,
much cleaner than it used to be.
It won't leave faint scum
on your skirted swimsuit
or your flabby thighs.
Its dark, sour smell
won't last, not
on your short hair.
A quick shampoo
will wash it off.
But you don't want to swim here.

The water is cool,
not cold like the ocean.
It sparkles warmly
like a snake in the sun.

The water is too cool.

Now the sand is damp,
even smooth.
No one pitches broken beer bottles
into this lake anymore
the night before the beach
opens for the season
and the kids' lessons start.

Still you don't want
to swim
here.

January Trees

Like ghosts of grandparents from the old country
waiting outside the kitchen window,

the trees stand while you scrub
last night's curry off heirloom plates.

The clarinet in your husband's klezmer
twines above you like a vine

whose few leaves and red berries
remain through January.

Birds fly between branches,
past empty nests,

last summer's twigs, threads, and paper.
Uninvited, the trees arrive early,

peering in as the sky turns the color
of their store-bought salad dressing,

not yours, not mine,
the color of the snow

that will not fall tonight.

Abandoned

June bamboo swallows
the bite-sized house. Sharp, green teeth
pierce darkness within.

Rooftop antenna
pulls in static. Red-winged black-
birds perch on its arms.

Humidity blooms
inside and out. Summer rain
curls up in the tub.

Paper coffee cups
clatter on bare floors. Dust
specks rise, caught in webs.

Empty hangers chat-
ter in the bedroom closet.
Bats greet another dusk.

Maryvale Park in July

The pond at the park clouds over.
Flies and fish kiss the water's surface.
Three birds dart through the air above.

Everywhere there is life in the water,
the reeds, the islands of brown-gray mud,
the flowers that crowd around the pond

as it shrinks and grows opaque. But
I cannot find the turtle I saw
last night. Squinting, holding my breath, I

glimpse it. But it does not move.
It is a turtle-shaped rock, mineral, not animal.
Bronze diamond, it will stay there forever.

I listen to the cicadas' twisting percussion,
look for flowering milkweed, and watch fireflies
like beads of sweat on hot nights.

Soon they too will die. Only sky,
earth, and water
will remain.

Seaweed on the Beach

Reds, greens, browns, and mustard yellow
add earthy undertones,
the taste of miso,
to the neons, the overexposed
blues and whites and yellows,
the painted plaques and t-shirts,
the stick candies and salt-water taffy
sold at the gift store.

The rusty Irish moss
on this beach
will not turn into
anemones or coral
or even amber sea glass.
It lingers like
the seagull accents
wheeling in the wind
past summer.

Looking Out to Spectacle Island in April

The beach this time of year
is nothing but rocks.
She ignores the man
who is placing one
on top of the other,
trying to balance them.

She ignores his dog.

She is waiting for the summer
of bare-chested boys in shallow water,
baseball on the radio,
and the reggae ice cream truck
with its flavors
of soursop, mango, and rum raisin.

She is waiting.

After Miles Davis' **Amandla**

Metallic trumpet
rises like heat mirages
over cracked asphalt.

Early morning drums
echo like the sidekick's fingers
on his closed window.

Eastern Oregon:
a blank land before breakfast.
Mountains are just haze.

Rainclouds hug the coast,
days away from this road trip.
Keyboards mimic rain.

It will not fall here.
Miles' trumpet scorches white
earth one cannot own.

The Day Before the Bridge Closed

On Boston's Long Island, I walk
over unmarked graves of residents,
now lost in earth and rocks,
hidden like they have always been
at this hospital, in their neighborhoods
before the city gentrified.

I stand at the island's edge,
looking out to waves, empty
space that smells of rot and
seaweed. The ragged tide rolls in
from Spain, leaving green sea glass
on this beach. Seagulls hover
over the prickly waves' unraveling,
over green shards worn smooth.
Tomorrow only ghosts will watch.

Birch Trees in North Carolina

The needle-thin trunks glint
the way the odd, white threads
do in a quilt of blues,
browns, and greens.

I do not recognize other trees,
but I know the birch.
Its peeled bark is snow
clinging to spring.
Its leaves are wind chimes.
Its roots clutch at the stone wall
between long-gone pasture
and forest.

I see this birch in Carolina,
not up north where I expected it,
but here among the rows
of oak and pine, beside
pools of water, part of
this quilt of sky, earth, and vine.

Savannah in January

Yearning for spring, I imagine
Spanish moss as white blossoms
bringing scent and warmth nearer.

I count bright green leaves
but find their waxy shade
impossible to bear in cold.

I seek snowdrops and crocus
but only see drowned camellias
closed to weak, winter sun.

Even here it's not time
for magnolias or cherry trees.
Flowers wait in vases, inside.

Today I circle the fountain
its edges trimmed with ice,
its trim painful to touch.

The Blooms of Fall

The sunburst's orange, rust and brown
burn into a turquoise door.
The last of the day lilies blanch
beneath this clash of color.

Hard green and white shields
armor the street tree.
The moss named British soldiers
musters in the bark below.

Tendrils cling to live oak,
the ghost of Walt Whitman,
lingering where young men at the college
sprawl, play ball, loiter, or loaf.

Other gray strands, the ghost of Li Bo,
dangle from a silver tree to the west.
In its shade, the red-haired scholar
memorizes poetry in Chinese.

A whole world in red, green, gray,
and orange blooms on pieces
of bark from trees fallen in silence,
on rocks made from the beginning of time.

In fall, in miniature, in moss and lichen,
another whole world is still blooming.

The Still Lives in Season

after Adriaen Coorte, "Still Life with Asparagus and Red Currants" (1696), "Still Life With Shells" (1696), "Shells" (1697), and "Asparagus" (1697)

Against the black absence of all light, presence of all color,
the painter in late spring arranges a dozen asparagus,
chalky white flushed with green, and a branch of
currants as red and translucent as glass beads in sunlight.

Come summer, white and pink shells unfold
like flowers whose perfume tastes salty, not sweet
in this ripe and rotten season. Dust hovers
over beetle-sized shells that harden and glint in the sun.

Winter's white conch spirals away
from the speckled and striped, the mottled pink and brown,
and into the day's light as thin and flat as a beach at low tide.
Absent all color, the conch points to the next season.

In spring, the painter again places white asparagus,
this time alone and enormous like an iceberg,
the lone survivor in its ocean, against
the same blackness as before.

Under the Sign of Ash

Just past solstice, we walk out
on Rock Creek Trail. Thin, brittle
ash trees crowd low mounds away
from both the path and water.

I recognize this tree. Its leaves
littered the pool even in summer.
Its branches shattered in spring breezes.
Fall purples and yellows muddied still,
warm waters.

On Rock Creek Trail, green dots
mark each trunk infested with ash
borers. These trees will be cut
down soon.

I imagine this trail without shade
in high summer. Together we watch
the thin creek flow. White bubbles,
the ghosts of leaves, float past.

I review my Celtic astrology. Ash
lives long, rises high, is grounded
by extensive roots. It shelters children.
Its wood becomes cradles. This is
not that world.

Rock Creek Park

Sirens weave a white web
around the park, containing it,
binding it to the city.

The rocks in this corner
were rejected by the builders.
They are the mistakes, the misshapen.

Wet, neon-green moss slides down
like boys' piss or spray paint
on the dull, marble blocks

that did not make it
to the blindingly white cathedral,
and the luminous monuments downtown

visited by tourists every day,
even in winter. These rocks stunt
the trees, even in summer

when other trees shade streets
near Georgetown. I expect poison
ivy to twine the park's

witchy trees or to crawl
onto the path. Without leaves
of three, the vine hides.

I expect to see Chandra
Levy's skeleton shattered behind
a stained stone, her hair

like a bird's nest matted
with twigs, dirt, and gravel,
her ghost warning all women,

even young crones like me,
to flee this winter landscape
of scattered stones and trees,

this park so distant from
the city where women can run
protected by sirens.

Blue Green and Brown (Rothko 1952)

She wonders what is intimate
about an enormous canvas hung
up on a museum wall.
Museums are silent except for
garbled conversations, docents' lectures, spills
of sound from someone's device.
Nothing is intimate, not even
silence, the pristine space between
each person in a public place.

She sits at home with
the image on her screen,
all other lights off. In
twilight, blue, green, and brown
envelop her, keeping her company
in this humidity. Cicadas call
outdoors. Indoor and outdoor sounds
blend: buses' wheeze, the washer's
slosh. She feels the space
between her and them dissolve.

Between Two Worlds

Between Two Worlds

After Yasuo Kuniyoshi's "Between Two Worlds" (1939)

Late afternoon hangs heavy with brown haze
the color of water from rusty pipes;
the ocean breeze does not cool.
Freed from Saturday at Woolworth's,
girls in high-waist khaki shorts
walk to the beach nonetheless.
It is no cooler anywhere else,
and they walk everywhere,
thighs muscling, the color
of the potatoes they do not eat .
Unwashed hair wrapped up
in haze-colored cotton scarves,
the girls stump through the sand
past beach grass, rocks,
a dead tree, and a bicycle tire.
They sniff out the boys
from the plant.
Inch by inch, foot by foot
in last year's shoes,
the girls make their way
to the hidden water,
cold ocean at low tide.
It will cleanse them and the boys.
The sky blisters, dark
clouds burning, about to
burst into flame
this summer
of nineteen thirty-nine.

Before the Last Days

She saw the mackerel sky
as shards clinging to blue.
Clouds gouged out her eyes.

The snow that could fall
burned like acid. She took
the path of least resistance

past the Viennese pastry shops
and travel agents with posters
in Hebrew, miles away from

the Rolling Stones' Manhattan. This
was Queens. "Shattered," the song
of old men, cycled through

her mind as she tore
into a bitter chocolate croissant.
The boss thought she waddled.

She marched down the subway
stairs into the smell of
excrement and money. Everyone else

was riding into Manhattan. She
was retreating further into Queens'
twilight on the tenth floor

where she waddled, short skirt
riding up her thighs. Longing

for the last days' burning,

she waited for the F-train.
Only three miles away,
the Hasidic ambulance pulled in.

She did not know that
the last days were already
here.

Coleus

Once again she sees these plants,
the ruffled red and green leaves,
the spiky purple flower, an afterthought
unlike roses, lilies, or crepe myrtle.

She is back in the faded
'80s, not the neon decade of
slicked-back hair and sunglasses at night,
but two years she spent looking
out third-floor windows past these plants.

She still smells this pissed-on street
from up there, the top floor
of a building that would burn
to the ground in ten years.

Five hundred miles away, the ashes
still catch in her throat.

At Low Tide

Already a ghost at twenty-three,
the singer Tim Buckley howls,
scaling octaves, stretching out syllables

until they dissolve in salty mist.
His fog of consonants and vowels,
salt and smoke, hovers, grazing

the skin of the dark-haired woman
standing by the window, holding
a candle in a baby-food jar.

Outside stairs to the second floor
quiver beneath keyboards and bass,
heavy footsteps of a ghost.

She turns away from the sea.
Cupping her hand around the
white flame, she blows out

her candle before the voice
breaks the last barrier
between indoors and out. Nobody

walks out on damp sands,
so far from cold water,
much further from yesterday's warmth.

Nobody walks out at low tide.
Even the seagulls dissolve
as if they were salt.

The woman at the window
has turned away. Her man
will not climb up to her,

not this morning, not tonight,
not when the fog wails
and salt embitters the air.

The Poet Charlotte Smith Drives Away

Her brain buzzing with botany,
backpack crammed with ungraded papers,
Charlotte wants to create a found poem,
transmuting the latest scientific research
from Memoirs of the New York Botanical Gardens
into poetry about lichen and peat mosses.

She crosses the quad,
contemplating the students
amongst the bricks and roses.
A girl in a sari tries
to sell her a samosa.
A grad student in a burkha
retreats to the library.
Charlotte holds her head high
and buys nothing.

She wants to write free verse
arguing against hiding
in cloth & custom
from the sunlit life.
There will be neither
lichen nor roses
nor research
in this poem.

Unburdened
by sari or burkha or skirt,
Charlotte in capri pants
hops into the driver's seat
and peels herself away.

She imagines writing
a poem for children
from the perspective
of a girl in a hijab.

A driver in a wig and micro mini
honks at her for traveling too slowly,
too thoughtfully on the highway.
Charlotte puts her sandaled foot down
and rockets towards home.

Somewhere further along,
past the clot of malls,
she merges into traffic,
and her mind returns to a sonnet
about a man shouting
at waves crashing
on an empty English shore.

She will write this one down
in her house like a beekeeper's hive,
one of many in a row
on the site of a fallow farm.
Her children will buzz around her
as bill collectors call.

The Poet of Spotsylvania

I scan the afternoon sky
for words, images, rhymes. Birds
take off from grasping trees
to fly south towards dolphins
and palms, towards warm ocean,
the direction I'm not going.

I want to stay home
where my yard grows all
the words, images, and rhymes
I need for my poems.
Nevertheless,

I get in my car
and drive north to work.
There strip malls bloom like
poison puffballs on far-off fields
that once grew sweet corn.

After work, I will not
see or hear the birds
sleeping in the barren trees.
My son will play videogames
behind a locked door. Gunfire

and tinny music will escape,
running upstairs to remind me
he's home. I'll go online
to visit the other poets
back from call centers, hospitals,
strip malls, and truck stops.

Then I'll write my poems.

Waleje for Caroline

I.
Gone to seed,
the onion flowers,
purple globes
erect in the wind
that, cooling,
promises rain soon,
no more endless summer.

II.
Banana and Louie bark,
recalling Caroline
to the tasks on her list:
wake the twins dress them feed them
get them into the car drive to the bank
drive to the strip mall buy cigarettes liquor stamps
drive to Lucky buy dog food people food kid food.

III.
Women from her grandmother's day
did not sweat. They glowed.
Her daughters will sweat,
playing tennis to win, lunging for the ball.
Caroline does neither.
Standing, chilled behind the picture window,
she lights a cigarette.

IV.
Caroline imagines the inland empire.
There the fields of onion flowers
extend in all directions
to the two-lane highway
to the forests to the mountains
to the other coast thousands of miles away.

She dreams of striding through these fields.

V.
Stabbing out her unsmoked cigarette,
Caroline turns away from the road
and towards the ocean.
She finger-combs her blonde hair,
too short for babies to yank.
Then she moves as if she were
already wading through saltwater.

VI.
Passing the photographs from Malibu,
she wonders if, like the onions,
she has gone to seed.
She sucks in her stomach
beneath her baggy blouse and shorts.
The dogs follow her.
She praises them but quickens her pace.

VII.
Walking down to the girls' room
with its windows on the beach,
she remembers
wearing yellow
blowing on dandelions
gone to seed
to bring on endless summer.

VIII.
Onion flowers bear with them
the tang of fall. She is now
three years past twenty,
two years a mother.

Come next spring, she promises
to show her twin daughters
dandelions.

IX.
Wagging their tails,
the dogs rush into her daughters' room.
The twins wake up for their friends.
Next spring she and the girls
will blow on dandelions gone to seed
to bring on endless summer
and the onion flowers of fall.

Evening on Washington Street

Walking where city blurs into suburb,
she sees yards of red roses
and orange lilies. Women her age
or older work in rich dirt
while grandchildren play.
Spanish phrases float
in the breeze around her.

Yet she smells nothing but the sweetness
of laundry detergent and fabric softener:
the choking purple fog of lavender grit.

Just off the path she rejected,
a green, peppery scent prevails.
There she could breathe deeply. But
she chose the known. She didn't
know where that path through woods
would have led her in twilight.

She knows the fog will dissolve
before she enters the square
and houses withdraw onto side streets.
She knows the white boxwood flowers
will smell like homemade soap,
cleansing the night as it falls.

Alternative History in Staunton, Virginia

The man who sings my favorite song
wanders the streets of this small city.
He no longer carries his guitar,
too heavy for walking past seventy
on uneven brick sidewalks
that all run uphill.

An ex-smoker,
he catches his breath
beneath the marquee
of the last one-screen movie theater,
the one that used to show
movies he liked.
It reeks of buttered popcorn.
He moves on

past the site
of the old Woolworth's,
the one that sold his records
back when they were hits,
when they crept out of open windows
even in this mountain town,

before they clung to him,
never leaving the room
with the reel to reel tape,
never leaving home.

The Last Days of Fusion

As saxophone and piano washed
past doorways, the couple walked
down the street, looking to
enter places they would have
never dared three years ago.

December snow fell in spurts.
She clenched, then unclenched gray
gloved hands in the pocket
of her teal wool coat.
His coat was new, too.

Already places were shutting down.
This was not New York,
not Manhattan. His friend Elgar
had died. So they couldn't
visit him in his three-decker,
too close to Harvard Square.

In the last days of fusion,
the couple walked on Mass Ave.,
avoiding their memories of Elgar,
nights they'd spent drinking tonic
and listening to Miles Davis
on crackling vinyl, to Elgar
cracking his jokes, telling his stories
about Cambridge in the Thirties.

Fine snow became light rain,
summoning the smell of damp wool.

A guitarist exited the cafe,
looking for his car as
the last trackless trolley fled
towards Trapelo Road. In doorways,
the young men played horns,
making the old songs fizz
like soda with lime.

Tonic

Chiefly Eastern New England: soda pop.

Morning thunderstorms keep us home,
away from swimming lessons and
the round of suburban errands.
Heavy, buggy clouds rumble;
lightning flashes beyond the pines.
Yesterday's humidity still clutches at us.

My mother sends my brother
to the basement to shut off
the electricity. The fan sputters,
then dies. We listen
to a transistor radio.
Jagged static interrupts
last summer's soft rock hits.
I sneak diet ginger ale
before it is tepid and flat.

Next summer I'll be working
for my father in the city
in the air-conditioned,
windowless office
on Dorchester Avenue.
Drinking icy cans of Pepsi
from the corner store,
listening to the Providence station,

I will imagine summer in Seekonk.
It blazes with classic rock
and feels as smooth as coconut oil
while storms keep my brother
and my mother home.

Visiting the Ancestors

The deer are visiting the ancestors,
nibbling on grass at Mt. Calvary,
waiting in the shade of winter

underneath the low trees that could be
on a riverbank in the deep
South that the ancestors fled from.

The five deer browse on the
pale green fringe of the cemetery,
limp parsley left on winter's plate

beside the river that neither flows
nor freezes. The deer have bodies
the color of earth in shadow,

but they could be spirit animals
of family living elsewhere come to
visit great-grandparents in the ground,

the great-grandfather who was gentle with
farm animals, remembered horses and mules,
the great-grandmother who kept a pot

on the stove for family, neighbors,
and friends, served Red Rose tea
with milk and sugar like coffee,

The deer linger on the fringes
like the awkward children they
once were when the ancestors

were alive.

Home from the Oncologist

Parking her car, Thelma counts the crows
balancing on the roof of her house.
The birds are almost as big as chimneys.

She tries to remember whether crows mean death.
No. Maybe owls or ravens are the auguries
out West where trees tower over houses.

But she knows Van Gogh's last painting,
the murder of crows in the cornfield
a day or two before he died.

She will ask her friends.
She cannot ask her husband.
He's been dead two years.

Thelma watches the crows fly
off to the neighbors' large house.
Crows are just birds up there.

On her roof they loomed like bad omens
from nights swirling with coal dust and
cigarette smoke, throbbing with nausea,

from another painting whose light
is just a smear of yellow and orange
oils trapped behind black lines.

She pictures her family's ghosts hovering
over her street, trying to find where she lives.
Once they find her, she must join them.

She must become like them,
dust and smoke mingling with crows,
whirling in blue sky over Vincent's wheat.

At Bonaventure Cemetery

after an image by Mary Judkins

At home in the world,
Spanish moss flows like sunlight
from the trees whose roots
are in fertile ground.
Sunlight hovers on the left
like the white light of myth,
movies, and musicals.

Today the ancestors walk among us,
recognizing the children in the adults,
laughing at the fashion
and gadgets we cherish.

Not at home in the world,
the mourning madonna hugs the cross,
but she is streaked with green.
Even the shadow striping her gown
is the color of soil, the red bricks
of the city beyond. Her tears
are moss, not the bitter crystal
that etches stained glass
and indoor stone.

The ancestors tiptoe around her,
but they mingle with us
in and out of sunlight,
in and out of shadow.

Listening to Robert Glasper

The last song
escapes your laptop
and rises just above your head.
A black man's voice fuzzes,
then disappears around
the brilliant corners.
With a flick of a switch,
the drum crisps.
The voice reappears.

Glasper remembers Nirvana's song.
You don't.

Other music blasted out
of the clothing stores
on Jamaica Ave. in Queens.
The hoop-earring girls
in neon leggings and high-tops
and lemon raspberry perfume
danced down the sidewalks
to "Gypsy Woman (She's Homeless)."
They were singing along with her
la da dee la dah dah.

Dressed for success
at your temp job,
you wanted to dance, too.
You did not.

Now you do.

Let's Go Away for Awhile

Thelma and her husband sing along to Pet Sounds
when driving to the Cape. Jerry Cole's guitar
begins "Wouldn't It Be Nice," and they launch

into song, his voice too wild, hers with
the Texas accent she never can lose. They
plunge in, splashing past strip malls and swamp.

But this instrumental is the song she loves best,
the vibraphone like sunshine against drums like surf,
the horns like the wave that crashes furthest

onto the rocks, not quite the highway.
The strings are clouds, meringue she has whipped
up in a stainless steel bowl at home.

She almost forgets that the east coast
has weak surf, and slimy seaweed clings to
waders' calves in warm, knee-high water

as she and her husband waddle in among
the thin girls from Boston. She then remembers
cold, cloudy Mondays when the two of them

drive back home, listening to their inland music:
Chicago blues, Texas swing, Hank Williams' Honky Tonkin',
the old songs that better suit their voices.

Maybe she likes that this instrumental comes before
anyone can see the bridge or the traffic.

Or she likes to catch her breath
before Sloop John B's lyrics grind her down
like the refrain of a whiny child.

She catches her breath.

The Jazz Harpist on a Sunday Afternoon

Fingers fly like sunlight
skimming the brightness
on the surface of the lake
one slightly breezy afternoon.

But here there are no words.
The sun is stepping down from its height.
It is still as lively
as the fingers of the harpist
plucking and stroking the strings
while the flute warbles its birdsong,
while her husband's drum spreads its branches,
upon which the flute and harp rest.

The anonymous tambourine shimmers
like the ice cubes
in the sun-lit, lemony drink
sweating on a table.
The lemony drink matches
the jazz harpist's shift
skimming an inch or two
above the knee.
The hand matches her crisp hair
that resists the breeze.

In the evening, there may be words,
shadows, a singing saxophonist
at the club downtown,
but for now,
for the harpist and her husband,
bathing in brightness,
there are none.

Always Looking at the Past, Sometimes Living by the River

Rocky Mountain High

I don't remember mountains in Denver.
I mistook them for clouds steeped
in shadow, soaked in wind, hugging

the horizon, limiting the distance of
our spectacled vision. Without a car,
the road through the mountains was

something to imagine, not to travel.
I remember walking wide streets, past
empty storefronts and flickering neon cacti.

Cutting through the university quad free
of weeds and students, we talked
about books we'd read and then

strolled to Safeway and the apartment.
I remember watching Seinfeld in black
and white. We drank Crystal Pepsi,

ate toasted bagels, the frozen kind,
smaller than my fist. Cynthia drew the
smoky drapes against night's noise, against

mountains in the distance, the future
of endless beginnings and false starts,
our late twenties, the nineteen nineties.

Returning to Jamaica Pond

On this cool day, sunlight
hides behind frayed clouds that
light turns translucent. Dank, green-
brown scent does not rise
from the opaque pond as
it did on warmer days.

After stepping off the outbound
trolley swaying into the future,
I once walked this pond
without stopping, without looking,
without reflecting.

Pausing for breath, I look
out to Turtle Island's rock
over which a dead tree
sprawls. This island is shrinking.
Rising waters will conceal it
long before the ocean covers
this growing city, my grave,
this shrinking grave, my city.

One Spring Morning at the Historic Icehouse

The perfect cube of ice descends.
Having wrapped it in plastic for protection,
volunteers are lowering it
into the historic icehouse.

The perfect cube chills this brick chamber
large enough for dozens of cubes
in the days before this icehouse
was historic, when no tourists
came to Florida.

Rough to the touch, red clay walls
protect this cube.
It will never melt.
The cube's chill keeps
mold and moss
from forming on the walls.

The icehouse smells of nothing
but cold, nothing
but straw and the dirt floor.
Unlike the zoo's dazed baby elephant
or the polar bear with yellowed fur,
it appeals to the tourists.

Lowering the perfect cube
by means of a historic hook and pulley,
the volunteers forget the thick air outside
as imperfect oranges and grapefruit spoil,
the corpse flower blooms,

and tourists' overheated cars
crawl past this historic site.

Shivering, not sweating,
the volunteers forget this spring morning,
these air-conditioned years.

Rothko on Portland Street

Rothko's paintings always make her think
of windows. She is sitting up
one evening in an East Cambridge kitchen,
hours past some man's bedtime, staring
at flat roofs and barbed-wire tangle,
a mile from the river. There
on day-glo afternoons kids her age
row the Charles after beef stir-fry
and before physics homework. She scrapes
butter into a bowl of brown
rice she had cooked, hoping he
would not miss even one grain.

Drinking tap water, wishing for soda,
she studies the Chinese Trees of Heaven
that spring up on Portland Street.
Rothko would have left them out
if he had been painting here.
They are too leafy, their triangles
disturbing the color blocks, their greens
disrupting the wash of orange paint.

Still the view makes her think
of Rothko, the poster she sees
at the college bookstore, the picture
on a book of poetry bought
elsewhere, closer to the river, to
read when she stays home alone.

The Space Between

She remembers riding, being driven
from county to county on state roads

two blue-black lanes cut through
cornfields, no houses, trees, or towns,

no radio or mixtape in the old car,
only their words, only talk.

Or maybe they did not like the same music.
He liked disco; she liked hip-hop.

Fifteen years after, she mourned John's death;
he did not even own one Beatles CD.

She didn't know what was there
beyond the car, the road, the books they'd read,

in-house gossip, the stars he knew but she didn't,
the drive to Indy or Champaign.

She didn't know about the trees
or the wildflowers she was not seeing.

To her friend, this was still the East,
only twenty-four hours' drive from the coast.

Having left home, she imagined that she was changing
going someplace different from where she had been.

She shook her newly red hair then.
She shakes her short brown hair now.

Back East again, she puts on her glasses
as if to see all that she had missed:

the abandoned farmhouses,
the yellow and red marigolds that outlast

trees and walls, crumbling brick towers,
people who emerge from whitewashed storefronts

in someone else's online photographs
of all that grows in the space between.

When Words Are Stones

Standing at the edge of the river,
she looks out at the caramel flood,

its thick, sweet color swelling over where
the stones were last summer. She remembers

seeing them for the first time, noticing
how bright the river was, how many

stones gathered around the stream like words
she could speak here with new friends

in this city, not her own. Choosing
a stone, feeling its dryness, its heat,

she considered whether to throw it or
to bring it to her room. Today

all stones are drowned in dirty water.
Today she has spoken to no one.

The river smells of mud, of drowned,
lost animals caught in the sudden flood

without branches to cling to. A leafless
tree stands aloof, branches out of reach

from water that laps at its roots.
This tree has survived each year's floods.

She turns away, knowing that the stones
will return, that words will, too. Tomorrow

she returns here whether the flood rises
or retreats. Next spring she will watch

it carrying away black branches and corpses
through the heart of this college town.

But today she returns home.

The Painter Dreams of Nevadaville, Colorado
after Yasuo Kuniyoshi's "Nevadaville" (1942)

Under the wind and smoke-bruised sky,
the brittle grass dances
as if it were ocean

lapping at the distant, gravel mountain.
The town's signs have faded,
becoming words seen only in dreams.

Before the war, the painter's
dreams took place in Nevadaville.
Then he used to travel to the shore

with his wife, the thick-waisted woman
who floated in the sea
like an ice cube in a tepid drink.

Before the war, he had never been
to a ghost town.   He lived
in New York City. He played golf.

After the war, he will dream
of Nevadaville, remembering this
ghost town where he forgot the ocean

and his wife who stayed
behind with the billowing waves,
not melting, not shrinking.

He will recollect the bruised sky,
the buildings like worn dice

thrown onto the matted grass,

his wife's body like vanilla
salt-water taffy, her red hair
streaming like seaweed,

all that he had tried to forget.

In Pale November

when I was Marianne Moore, wearing a black straw hat,
we wandered through the woods he knew too well.

Leafless trees clutched at the faded sky.
Stones and fallen branches littered the ground.

I listened to his youthful harangue
and watched for birds and plants she would have seen,

but it was long past time for even poison ivy
or bittersweet berries. So he and I drifted

until the early dark pooled at our feet
to freeze and trip us like the branches, stones,

and fallen leaves that always cling to pale November.
For years beginning with that month,

I listened to his middle-aged litany and ignored
the leather-bound books she wove into her poetry,

following the sound of his voice
into and through the woods and out the other side

to the early darkness, the evergreen trees,
the stray cats, the bus stop signs like clenched fists,

to the long ride on empty buses
back to the city we always returned to.

Walking through Rock Creek Park in November,
having left the city I always returned to,

I count syllables the way she did.
I try to remember his voice.

For My Ex-Husband's Twin Sons
Summer 1996

That summer we still believed in astrology.
Anything could happen. I could learn to drive
stick shift. The Indian astrologer predicted that
my soon-to-be ex-husband would father twin sons,
mother unknown.

All summer stringy-haired women wandered
in and out of the apartment. The hems
of their long skirts were as frayed
as my marriage was. The women brought
bruised fruit and scotch-taped paperbacks of esoteric
philosophy stinking of patchouli. Home from work,
I drank Café Bustelo with whole milk.
One woman stood barefoot in the backyard,
warning me about the man I liked.
All she needed to know was his
birth date.

I imagined driving away with Balzac's novels
in my trunk. I popped the clutch
and went nowhere.

The Last Summer without Air Conditioning

She sits on the porch
between the house and barn
with the friend who would
have been her landlady.

They sip OK Soda
from garnet goblets
as sun retreats into clouds
far from sunset or skyline.

The smell of grilled steak
rises from over the fence.
The Macarena bursts forth
from a car on Centre Street.

The neighbor with tiny glasses
slams his upstairs window shut.
His black guitar grinds and shrieks.
His mastiff howls.

The women pick at their salad
of dandelion greens
and avocado.
They will talk later.

She pretends that she can't
see her ex
ambling up the driveway,
but she can,

even over the gnash of guitar.

She pretends that she can't
see the city
that she is leaving,
but this is it,

the city that she is leaving.

For My Ex-Husband's Twin Sons
Summer 1997

The next summer I believed in nothing.
Windows open, drinking icy Pepsi, with the fan off,
I lay awake upstairs, not reading *Clarissa*
while my friend the atheist slept
in the basement to escape the heat
while the man I liked slept
back in the city I'd left.

As I listened to the oldies from Battle Ground,
I thought nothing would change. I had
been listening to these songs for years.
Levi Stubbs would always plead to Bernadette.
Dusty would always offer advice I'd never take.
Alone in bed, I would be reading
these thick books forever,
my life captured in small print
and amber-colored soda
drunk in some college town.
Like *Clarissa*, this life would continue
as long as I chose to turn the page.

This was the summer you two could have
been born, perhaps to a stringy-haired woman
who had traipsed in and out of our apartment,
perhaps to a fierce woman in red.
For her, whether or not she kept you,
whoever she once was,
everything would have changed.

Ms. Hawthorn

dreams of standing on a ridge in Britain,
looking down on cathedrals and car parks,
on pubs and Morris dancers,
albums she knew from
used record stores and
long-lost friends' collections.

Dirty blonde hair
streaming in the wind,
she would be barefoot,
wear white, in spite
of mud and wet grass.

At fifty, she sits in traffic.
Through mousy- brown bangs,
she blinks at mist
falling on her windshield,
the line of cars
snaking on past the exit.

As violins on the CD swell,
a young man sings
about growing older
on a morning like this one.
He has just arrived in town;
she has lived in this state
for a dozen years.

Narrow

In this part of the country,
windows narrow,

squeezing sunlight into the bedroom
as if it were lemon juice.

In this part of the country,
porches are tiny.

One plant in its terra cotta pot
stands in for coleus and marigolds,

for woods behind the house,
for vacant lots full of Queen Anne's Lace.

In this part of the country,
black cats race down brick alleys.

There is no room for grass
or children.

At Mile Zero on SR 26

The open road unspools
like a fresh typewriter ribbon
before even one smack
of a noiseless key
onto heavy, white paper.

You forget that you hate
typewriters, especially
inserting a new ribbon.

Turn on the radio.
Stations weave in
and out
like drivers in city traffic.

You'd settle for silence,
but then the old song
you love best
staggers in beside you,
keeping you company
on the road home.

The Summer After the Bridge Closed

In the absence of lawn mowers, the sparrow's
song flows down slate tiles,
over brick walls and wooden window sills
to the rocks at island's edge.

Fat black crows strut down
quiet streets, across matted grass.
Without hawks or humans,
crows have no need to fly.

Waves crash onto smaller stones
that gather next to the rocks.
The ocean's fingers crumble
the beach as if it were a cracker.

For now, starlings emerge
from rhododendrons and boxwoods.
The birds' notes replace the rain
during this dry summer.

The grass is greener. Clover
mingles with chicory and milkweed.
Long grass sways in the wind.
It flowers.

Dreams of Lafayette

St. Boniface's narrow, slate spire
punctures the clouds in the sky.
Inside these apartments grad students
read literary theory. Espresso machines
rattle and Diet Coke chills.
A couple calmly speaks French.
His blue bike waits outside.
It is ready for him
to leave this Hoosier city
for someplace on the coast.

Trains shook our wooden house
on Ferry Street every night.
I would dream of earthquakes
shattering windows and ceilings crumbling
in apartments I once lived in.
When we couldn't get back
to sleep, we graded papers.
We drove to the all-night Village
Pantry across Sixth Street's tracks.

Now the trains are gone,
rerouted beyond the highway and
strip malls. The Village Pantry
closes at ten. I dream
of Lafayette, living in these
sturdy buildings, strong enough to
protect us and our child.
The bike, the one color,
the metallic shimmer of sky
in this black and white
world, is yours.

I Don't Remember the Willamette
Response to Bea Garth's painting "At the River" (2012)

If I were to paint a picture of my life in Oregon,
that river would not run through it.

I remember moss growing on tree trunks, the sequoia trees
dwarfing brown, flat-roofed houses,
the first camellias and azaleas I saw,
their tissue-pinks dissolving in the warm rain,
the city limits, the two mountains like the head and foot of a bed.

I started to climb Spencer's Butte in a handmade sundress and sneakers.
Our friends in shorts wore hiking boots and carried water.
I thought of Mt. Washington's whipping wind, the last time
I had stood on a treeless summit, waiting for the van
to drive us back down while an icy rain pricked through the sleeve of
my orange coat. The two of us drank ginger ale and headed home.

I remember following the Amazon Creek to pick wild blackberries
on Sundays when the buses did not run to campus.

I remember the McKenzie River, dipping my hand in soapy water.
So far from the city, I had expected something crystal, something drinkable.

I remember the dry mountains in the distance that no one climbed.
I still dream of driving past them to towns I never visited:
Junction City. Tangent. Sweet Home. Albany.
Places my students came from. Places my friends did not.

I remember when Jesse Nash drowned. Thrown from his inner tube,
the young athlete had no chance as the Willamette,
true to its Kalapuyan name, rippled and sped past the rocks.

I remember Interstate 5. Like a river, it ran past fields of rye-grass
on to Corvallis, on to Portland, then out of state.

Set by the farmers, fires hid the mountains from us in the city.
Some of us at home choked on the smoke. Others on the road
were killed. We wanted to be anywhere else on those days,
to be back home where these bonfires had been banned.

But I do not remember the Willamette.

Riding into Charles Street Station

In response to Joan Dobbie's "A City Wears Its River Like a Necklace."

The river wasn't yet someone else's necklace.
I glimpsed it on my way to work,
looking up from a book my boss had given me
about someone else's city.

Crew teams were scuttling home down the silver river
to breakfast and their first class, the mathematics
that would have freed me from electric typewriter
and telephone, from this two-hour commute
that ended at the ocean, the calculus
that would have kept me from
my residents and coworkers at Long Island Hospital.

I imagined walking alongside the river,
even just crossing it on foot
in sunlight that glittered on the water
like glass, like borrowed costume jewelry
and in the sunset that would stain it orange.

I imagined living near the river,
perhaps in the building I saw
right before entering the tunnel.
I would grow used to the sight of
trains before midnight and the black waters
after. The river would stay in my mind
the way that my aunt's gift of pearls did,
kept for special occasions, therefore
never worn.

But the river was always someone else's necklace.
A dumpy girl in nylons and pastels, not
dressed for success, not even wearing earrings,

I was passing through on a subway car
that was often filled with other riders
blocking my view of the river.
Most of them had a better right
to this necklace than I did.

I was biding my time, waiting
to leave for some other city,
some other river that I could
touch and taste and smell,
a river that was not jewelry.

Lafayette, September 11, 2001

Later that morning after classes were cancelled,
I crossed the river, beneath a perfect sky,
going home to you.

We didn't think that Al-Qaeda would reach us
in this college town,
this pin that the angels danced on.

We listened to the radio.

We thought about stopping by your parents'.
There your mother watched the news all day
as if it were the rain that would not fall.

Instead I watched the trucks trailing American flags
rush up and down Ferry Street,
making it a river we could not cross.

I wished it had rained that morning
while the passengers were lining up at Logan
and the workers were streaming from the subway.

Standing at the window, looking at the sky,
fierce even in Lafayette,
city of wedding-cake houses and candy stores,

I prayed for rain.

Acknowledgements

The author gratefully acknowledges the following journals and anthologies where earlier versions of these poems have appeared:

Anti-Heroin Chic – "Ms. Hawthorn"
Black Poppy Review – "At Bonaventure Cemetery," "Visiting the Ancestors"
Cactifur – "What I Found Among the Reeds" and "Rocky Mountain High"
Contemporary American Voices – "Let's Go Away for Awhile" and "One Spring Morning at the Historic Icehouse"
Duane's PoeTree – "The Summer After the Bridge Closed"
Eos: The Creative Context – "Dreams of Lafayette," "The Last Days of Fusion," and "The Last Days without Air Conditioning," "I Don't Remember the Willamette" and "Riding into Charles Street Station"
Figroot Press – "Under the Sign of Ash" and "Before the Last Days"
Firefly Literary Journal – "The Day Before the Bridge Closed"
Fourth and Sycamore – "January Trees"
Flutter Poetry Journal – "Maryvale Park in July"
Indiana Voice Journal – "Home from the Oncologist" and "The Poet of Spotsylvania"
Indie Soleil Magazine – "Rothko on Portland Street"
Ink in Thirds – "At Mile Zero on SR 26"
Jellyfish Whispers – "Looking Out to Spectacle Island in April"
ken again -- "She Wonders What Will Become of This City"
The Literary Nest – "Birch Tree in New England" (as "Birch Tree")
Literature Today – "Visiting the Ancestors" (as "The Visitors")
Mad Swirl – "Alternative History in Staunton, VA," "To Eat the Rowan's Fruit" and "For My Ex-Husband's Twin Sons (Summer 1996)" (as "For My Ex-Husband's Twin Sons (1)")
Of/with – "After Yasuo Kuniyoshi's Between Two Worlds (1939)," "At the Water's Edge," "The Blooms of Fall," "Rock Creek Park," "Waleje for Caroine," "Listening to Robert Glasper," and "Sophia, What Might Have Been"
Peeking Cat Poetry Magazine – "At Low Tide"
Plum Tree Tavern – "The Drought Close to Home"
Poppy Road Review – "The Still Lives in Season"
Quill and Parchment – "Evening on Washington Street"

Rasputin – "For My Ex-Husband's Twin Sons (Summer 1997)"

Red Bird Chapbooks' Weekly Read – "Lafayette, September 11, 2001"

The San Pedro River Review – "Nature on the Other Side of the Glass"

Setu – "Blue Green and Brown (Rothko 1952)"

Silver Birch Press – "In Pale November"

Snapping Twig – "We Disaster Tourists Travel to the Salton Sea"

Solidago Journal – "Narrow" and "Coleus"

South Florida Literary Journal – "Easter 2116"

Taj Mahal Literary Review – "Crepe Myrtle in East Rockville"

Tipton Poetry Journal – "When Words Are Stones"

Truck – "The Space Between"

Walking is Still Honest – "Returning to Jamaica Pond"

The Wild Word – "After Miles Davis' Amandla" and "Tonic"

Yellow Chair Review – "Mother at the Town Beach"

Young Ravens Literary Review – "Savannah in January" (as "Yearning for Spring")

"Abandoned" appeared in *Write Like You're Alive* (Zoetic Press, 2016).

"At the Library of Water" and "The Library of Air" appeared in *Element(ary) My Dear* (Kind of a Hurricane Press, 2015).

"The Jazz Harpist on a Sunday Afternoon" appeared in *Switch (the Difference)* (Kind of a Hurricane Press, 2015).

"The Painter Dreams of Nevadaville, Colorado" appeared in *Secrets and Dreams* (Kind of a Hurricane Press, 2016).

"Seaweed on the Beach" appeared in *Of Sun and Sand* (Kind of a Hurricane Press, 2013).

"Home from the Oncologist" appeared in *Resurrection of a Sunflower* (Pski's Porch Publishing, 2017)

"At Bonaventure Cemetery" was nominated for a Pushcart Prize

Pski's Porch Publishing was formed July 2012, to make books for people who like people who like books. We hope we have some small successes. **www.pskisporch.com**.

323 East Avenue
Lockport, NY 14094
www.pskisporch.com

21364536R00061

Made in the USA
Columbia, SC
17 July 2018